D1070851

Earthquake in Loma Prieta, California, 1989

Susan and William Harkins

Mitchell Lane
PUBLISHERS

P.O. Box 196
Hockessin, Delaware 19707
Visit us on the web: www.mitchelllane.com
Comments? email us: mitchelllane@mitchelllane.com

Printing   1   2   3   4   5   6   7   8   9

A Robbie Reader/Natural Disasters
Earthquake in Loma Prieta, California, 1989
The Fury of Hurricane Andrew, 1992
Mt. Vesuvius and the Destruction of Pompeii, A.D. 79
Mudslide in La Conchita, California, 2005
Tsunami Disaster in Indonesia, 2004
Where Did All the Dinosaurs Go?

Library of Congress Cataloging-in-Publication Data
Harkins, Susan Sales.
    Earthquake in Loma Prieta, California, 1989 / by Susan and William Harkins.
       p. cm. — (Natural disasters — what can we learn?)
    "A Robbie Reader."
    Includes bibliographical references and index.
    ISBN 1-58415-417-9 (library bound : alk. paper)
    1. Loma Prieta Earthquake, Calif., 1989—Juvenile literature. 2. Earthquakes—
    California—Juvenile literature. I. Harkins, William. II. Title. III. Series.
       QE535.2.C18H37 2005
       363.34'95'097946—dc22
                                                                          2005010061

ABOUT THE AUTHORS: Susan and Bill Harkins live in Kentucky and they enjoy writing together for children. Susan has written many books for adults and children. Bill is a history buff and helps Kentuckians prepare for earthquakes and other natural disasters as a member of the Civil Air Patrol.

PHOTO CREDITS: Cover: Chuck Macke/Getty Images; p. 4 Jamie Kondrchek; p. 6 Otto Greule, Jr./Getty Images; p. 8 Jamie Kondrchek; p. 10 Otto Gruele, Jr./Getty Images; p. 12 Jamie Kondrchek; p. 14 Getty Images; p. 16 Otto Gruele, Jr./Getty Images; p. 18 Jonathan Nourok/Getty Images; p. 20 D. Parker/Photo Researchers, Inc.; p. 22 Photo Researchers, Inc.; p. 24 James McClanahan/courtesy Caltech Archives; p. 25 James King-Holmes/ Photo Researchers, Inc.; p. 26 Adam Teitelbaum/Getty Images; p. 27 Jonathan Nourok/ Getty Images

TABLE OF CONTENTS

Words in **bold** type can be found in the glossary.

If you're indoors during an earthquake, crawl under a large piece of furniture, like the kitchen table, where dangerous objects can't fall on you. Then, cover your head with your hands.

SHAKE, RATTLE, AND ROLL!

"Mom! Toby peed on me!" I cried as my cat shot across the living room floor. Just then, I heard a low rumble. The house began to shake. "**Earthquake!**" (URTH-qwake) I shouted.

My legs wobbled. I couldn't stand up to run. Quickly, I crawled into the kitchen and got under the table. The floor rocked under me. It was like being in my father's small boat out on San Francisco Bay. My grandmother's old clock began to chime.

"Cover your head!" Mom shouted.

Water splashed from a pot onto the hot stove. Mom held on to the counter. She

Earthquakes are noisy. People often say an earthquake sounds like loud thunder. You might hear things falling around you. The sound of this building collapsing must have been deafening.

reached to turn off the burner. Knives and forks bounced on the table over my head. Whole onions and potatoes rolled to the floor. The screen door slammed again and again.

The rumbling grew. It sounded like thunder coming from under the ground.

Canisters fell over. They dumped coffee, sugar, and flour everywhere. Cooking oil cut a river through the mess.

The rumble swelled into the loudest, most terrifying roar I'd ever heard.

A chunk of plaster fell from the ceiling. It exploded at my mother's feet. Overhead, something pelted the roof. Was the roof going to collapse on us?

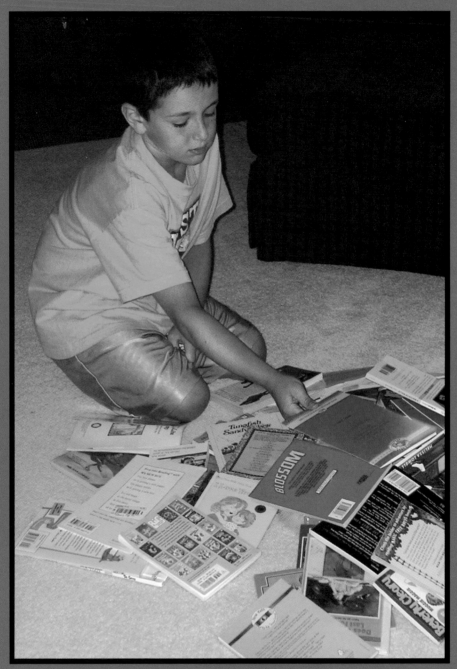

Cleaning up after an earthquake can take a while. If you're lucky, you may only have to put things back where they belong.

THE SHAKING STOPS

Suddenly, it was quiet and still. The air was full of dust. Or was it flour?

I was too afraid to move. Mom rushed to me. "Are you hurt?" she asked. I was so scared I wanted to cry.

That's when we heard meowing. "Toby!" I shouted. We found our cat under a pile of books in the living room. He was scared, but he wasn't hurt. Now I understood why he had peed on me. Animals often behave strangely before an earthquake.

"Your dad!" Mom gasped. Dad was at the 1989 World Series baseball game in Candlestick Park. The ballpark is located in San Francisco. Dad's ticket had been a treat from his boss for working hard all summer.

After the earthquake, trapped baseball fans at Candlestick Park waited. Eventually, the police **evacuated** (ee-VAA-kyoo-ay-ted) the stadium.

I turned on the television but the power was out. Mom got a busy signal when she called Dad's cell phone. The phone lines were jammed.

Mom stepped over the gooey flour-and-oil mess. She walked to the back door. For the first time ever, the screen door was shut tight. She had to push the handle hard to open it.

The backyard was soaked. Nearly a foot of water had splashed out of the swimming pool. We walked around the side of the house. The chimney lay in a crumbled heap. The falling bricks must have been what we'd heard hitting the roof during the earthquake. We stepped over the bricks and walked around front.

The house across the street had moved, but its concrete (KON-kreet) porch hadn't budged. It looked strange.

For a moment, I wanted to run away. But where would I be safe? Mom hugged me and I felt better. Waiting with Mom for Dad to come home was the safest place for me to be.

An earthquake kit should contain emergency equipment such as a flashlight, extra keys, money, batteries, water, and a radio.

WE START TO REACT

"We need our earthquake kit!" I said.

We hurried back inside our house. We opened the door to the closet under the stairs. The kit was in a strong box on wheels. The box held a first aid kit, flashlights, batteries, a radio, blankets, food, a **fire extinguisher** (FIRE eck-STING-gwih-shur), and toilet paper. A smaller box had money, keys, a list of phone numbers, and a checklist. There were bottles of fresh water in the closet too.

"We are very lucky," Mom said. "We only need the radio right now."

The Loma Prieta earthquake was so strong that roads cracked and bridges collapsed. The top level of Interstate-880, above, fell onto lower levels.

She read the checklist. First, we smelled all over the house for gas leaks. We didn't find any. Second, we tried to call Aunt Mia in Nevada (nuh-VAH-duh) to let her know we were all right. Mom couldn't get through. Third, we checked the tap water. Good news! We had running water. Mom said we shouldn't drink it until we knew that it was safe.

We went back outside to check on our neighbors. Mr. Mendez was watching the news on a battery-powered television. He invited us to watch too. Soon, many of our neighbors were standing around the little television.

I will never forget what I saw on the news that evening. The top layer of a double-decker highway had fallen. People in cars on the lower level were crushed. Later, we saw a big bridge where one section had collapsed.

Finally, I saw what I'd been waiting for. They showed the baseball stadium where my dad was supposed to be. The stadium was okay. A reporter was talking about the damaged roads. How would my dad get home?

"Your dad will be home soon, even if he has to walk," Mom said. She reminded me that Dad had an emergency kit in the trunk of his car. That made me feel better.

Emergency workers take special care to make sure buildings don't completely collapse.

WAITING

It was getting dark, but we were afraid to go inside. **Aftershocks** (AF-tur-shokz) can be almost as bad as the earthquake. It was warm for October, so we stayed outside.

In the darkness, we saw a glow in the sky. Someone said that there was a bad fire across the bay. We heard sirens in the distance. I snuck away with some friends. We climbed on a roof to watch the fire.

My mother was mad when she found me. She scolded me in front of my friends. She never does that. But she was right. If I had been sitting on the roof when an aftershock hit, I could have fallen. Or the roof could have

Sometimes, emergency workers allow people to return to their damaged homes to remove personal items and valuables. It is dangerous to enter a building damaged by an earthquake without official permission.

collapsed. I wasn't thinking when I climbed on that roof.

I apologized to Mom. She cooked hot dogs on our grill. While we ate, Mr. Mendez played his guitar. I asked if he would teach me a song. He showed me how to play a few **chords** (KORDS). Soon I was strumming and singing "Yankee Doodle." Just then, I heard somebody say, "Well, I'll be a doodle dandy!" I looked up and saw Dad!

Mom and I nearly knocked him down with our hugs. He laughed and Mom cried. I started to cry too, just a little.

Everyone spent that night in tents. All those tents lined up along the street made a funny sight. No one slept much though, not even Toby. There were many scary aftershocks that night.

The power was back on the next morning. It took all day to clean up, but we didn't mind. We felt lucky because none of us got hurt. We could rebuild the chimney. Not everyone was as lucky as we were.

Sometimes a fault looks like a huge crack in the earth. You can't see all faults from the surface of the earth. Some are underground.

JUST THE FACTS

We learned what happened when we went back to school. Our teachers explained that the earth's surface sits on huge underground "islands" called **tectonic** (tek-TON-ik) **plates.** These plates are several miles under the earth's surface. Sometimes they slam into one another or they slide away from each other. When that happens, we have an earthquake.

The place where two plates meet is known as a **fault** (FAWLT). A fault is like a giant crack in the earth. My family lives near the San Andreas (SAN an-DRAY-us) Fault in California. It's a big crack that runs north and south through most of the state. The North American Plate is on the east of the fault. The Pacific Plate is on the west.

You might think that living on top of one of the biggest cracks in the world is scary, but it isn't so bad. We have earthquakes all the time. Most of them are small. We barely even notice them. But at 5:04 P.M. on October 17, 1989, we had a big one. The Pacific Plate jumped north and generated a major earthquake. When the plate stopped, it was six feet closer to Oregon (OR-uh-gon) and four feet higher than the North American Plate next to it.

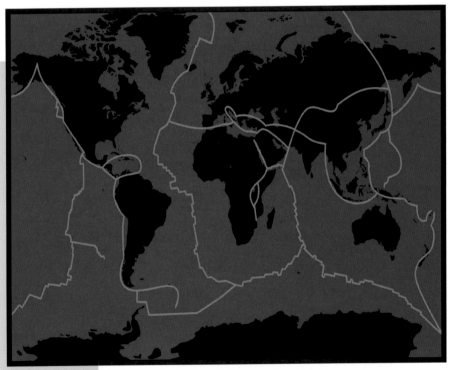

These red lines show the earth's major fault lines. Can you find the San Andreas Fault in California?

The earthquake happened 11 miles under **Loma Prieta** (LO-ma pree-EH-tuh) Peak in the Santa Cruz Mountains. That's why we call it the Loma Prieta earthquake. It was close enough to San Francisco, Oakland, and other cities to cause a lot of damage:

- At least 66 people died.

- 3,757 people were hurt.

- It cost $6 billion to repair the damage.

- A huge fire destroyed or damaged many buildings in San Francisco's Marina (ma-REE-nuh) District.

- The Cypress Street Viaduct (VIE-uh-dukt), a portion of the Nimitz Freeway (I-880), collapsed. Forty-two drivers and passengers were killed.

- A 50-foot section of the San Francisco-Oakland Bay Bridge collapsed. One driver was killed.

- Portions of several other freeways collapsed.

- More than a thousand landslides and rockfalls blocked traffic.

Seismologists study the shockwaves produced by earthquakes to determine their strength. A seismologist, shown here, studies a seismograph.

People all over California and even in Nevada felt the earthquake that day. That wasn't the only time the earth shook. There were more than 87 aftershocks over the next three weeks. Aftershocks aren't as strong as the earthquake, but they can still cause damage.

We can't **predict** (pre-DIKT) earthquakes. Special scientists called **seismologists** (size-MAH-luh-jists) study earthquakes to learn more about them. These scientists use charts made by a machine called a **seismograph** (SIZE-moe-graf). Seismographs measure earthquakes all over the earth. Seismologists carefully study the seismographic charts.

After an earthquake, seismologists use the charts to determine the earthquake's size, or **magnitude** (MAG-nih-tood). They plug the data from the seismographic charts into a set of special tables and charts known as the **Richter** (RICK-tr) scale. Scientists named this scale after the scientist who created it, Charles Richter.

Charles Richter studied earthquakes and developed a scale to measure their strength. Here he looks at a seismograph that he kept in his living room.

Not all buildings collapse. Sometimes a building slides off its foundation and crushes everything in its path.

Using the Richter scale, an earthquake's magnitude has a value between 1 and 10. A 2 earthquake is 10 times stronger than a 1. A 3 earthquake is 10 times stronger than a 2, and 100 times stronger than a 1. Each time the value increases by one whole number, the magnitude increases 10 times.

Most earthquakes are a 3 or less. We don't even notice them. Anything over a 5 can cause some damage. The Loma Prieta earthquake of 1989 measured 7.1 on the Richter scale. The strongest earthquake ever

Often, earthquakes cause so much damage that a building can't be repaired. When that happens, specially trained crews tear down the building.

known was a 9. As far as we know, there has never been a 10. An earthquake over 10 is possible, though not likely.

Seismologists also use seismographic charts to help them guess where earthquakes are most likely to happen. That helps people prepare for them by building stronger buildings and highways. We can't stop earthquakes, but we can be ready for them.

CHRONOLOGY

October 17, 1989, 5:00 P.M. Pacific Time

Baseball fans in Candlestick Park in San Francisco, California, wait for the opening of the third game in the 1989 World Series between the San Francisco Giants and the Oakland Athletics. People all over the world tune in to watch the game. Without warning, ABC loses their signal, leaving the world to watch static. No one knows it yet, but the viewers just witnessed the first few seconds of a 7.1 earthquake, centered 11 miles beneath Loma Prieta Peak in the Santa Cruz Mountains.

October 17, 1989, 5:04 P.M.

A 50-foot section of the San Francisco-Oakland Bay Bridge's upper deck collapses onto the deck below.

October 17, 1989, 5:04 P.M.

People living near Interstate-880 watch as section after section of the freeway collapses, tumbling like a huge wave across the landscape. Many people rush to the highway to assist those trapped under the fallen concrete. They begin to climb 30 feet up to the trapped commuters. These brave rescuers cover their faces with handkerchiefs and rags to protect themselves from cement dust and acrid smoke from the burning cars. They search for hours, going from car to car, looking for survivors.

October 17, 1989, 5:10 P.M.

Oakland Fire Engine No. 5 is the first to arrive at the I-880 freeway after seeing the dust and smoke rising from the debris. The firemen are unable to radio in a report because the communications system is overloaded.

October 17, 1989, 5:10 P.M.

The first call reporting I-880's collapse comes in at the Oakland Fire Dispatch Center.

October 17, 1989, 5:44 P.M.

Baseball commissioner Fay Vincent suspends the World Series. Power is out at Candlestick Park, so the announcer uses a battery-powered bullhorn to ask the fans to go home. On their way out, fans see a tall column of smoke rising from the Marina District.

October 17, 1989, about 5:50 P.M.

A broken gas main explodes in the Marina District, starting a major fire. A broken water main forces firefighters to draw water from a lagoon to fight the fire.

October 17, 1989, 6:00 P.M.

The city's fireboat arrives in the Marina Harbor. Neighborhood volunteers haul the hoses from the fireboat.

October 18, 1989, 2:00 A.M.

A radio broadcast reports that a tsunami has wiped out a block of Oceanside businesses. Later, the report is proved false.

October 18, 1989

San Francisco's *Chronicle* exaggerates casualties with the morning headline "Hundreds Dead in High Quake."

October 21, 1989

Buck Helm, a victim of the I-880 collapse, is found alive after being buried 4 days. His chest is crushed, he has a mild skull fracture, and his kidneys are failing from dehydration. He is conscious and waves to bystanders.

October 21, 1989

President George Bush visits the destruction of I-880.

October 27, 1989

The Oakland Athletics win the third game of the 1989 World Series in Candlestick Park.

October 29, 1989

A memorial service for the victims of the I-880 collapse is held in Oakland at Liberty Hall.

November 18, 1989

The Bay Bridge reopens.

November 19, 1989

Buck Helm dies of injuries sustained when the Cypress Street Viaduct section of I-880 collapsed. In that collapse alone, 42 people died. In all, the Loma Prieta quake claimed at least 66 lives.

WORLD'S DEADLIEST EARTHQUAKES
IN RECENT HISTORY

Date	Location	Deaths	Magnitude
1908	Italy	up to 100,000	7.2
1920	China	200,000	7.8
1923	Japan	143,000	7.9
1927	China	200,000	7.9
1932	China	70,000	7.6
1935	Pakistan	up to 60,000	7.5
1948	Turkmenistan	110,000	7.3
1970	Peru	66,000	7.9
1976	China	at least 255,000	7.5
1990	Iran	50,000	7.7
2004	Sumatra	283,000	9.0
2005	South Asia	over 31,000	7.6

FIND OUT MORE

Books

Harrison, David L. *Earthquakes: Earth's Mightiest Moments.* Honesdale, Pennsylvania: Boyds Mills Press, 2004.

Osborne, Mary Pope. *Earthquake in the Early Morning.* New York: Random House Books for Young Readers, 2001.

Sherrow, Victoria. *San Francisco Earthquake, 1989: Death and Destruction.* Berkeley Heights, New Jersey: Enslow Publishers, 1998.

On the Internet

American Red Cross: Earthquake Page
http://www.redcross.org/services/disaster/ 0,1082,0_583_,00.html

Earthquake Facts and Earthquake Fantasies
http://earthquake.usgs.gov/bytopic/megaqk_facts_fantasy.html

Federal Emergency Management Agency Disaster Preparedness for Kids
http://www.fema.gov/kids/

Life Along the Faultline
http://www.exploratorium.edu/faultline/index.html

Putting Down Roots in Earthquake Country
http://www.earthquakecountry.info/roots/roots.html

USGS Earthquake Hazards Program – For Kids Only
http://earthquake.usgs.gov/4kids/

GLOSSARY

aftershocks — (AF-tur-shokz)—smaller earthquakes that follow a major earthquake.

chords — (KORDS)—several musical tones that are played at the same time.

earthquake — (URTH-qwake)—the shock that results when the earth's tectonic plates collide or slide apart.

evacuated — (ee-VAA-kyoo-ay-ted)—emptied the area completely.

fault — (FAWLT)—a giant crack in the earth where two tectonic plates meet; earthquakes can happen along faults.

fire extinguisher — (FIRE eck-STING-gwih-shur)—a device used to put out fires.

Loma Prieta — (LO-ma pree-EH-ta)—the name of a peak in the Santa Cruz Mountains in California. The phrase means "dark hill" in Spanish.

magnitude — (MAG-nih-tood)—an earthquake's size or strength.

predict — (pre-DIKT)—to try to guess the future.

Richter scale — (RICK-tr)—a scale from 1 to 10 used to measure an earthquake's strength, devised by Charles Richter.

seismograph — (SIZE-moe-graf)—a machine that measures and records vibrations in the earth.

seismologists — (size-MAH-luh-jists)—scientists who study earthquakes.

tectonic plates — (tek-TON-ik)—huge "islands"under the earth's surface that move.

INDEX